Junk-Food Finders

middle of 2nd grade

Karen O'Connor

Illustrated by Glen Meyers

For Noah, Johannah, and Jacob

ACTION READERS

**Junk-Food Finders
Little-Kids' Olympics
French Toast and Dutch Chocolate
Service with a Smile**

Unless otherwise noted, Scripture quotations are taken from the HOLY BIBLE, NEW INTERNATIONAL VERSION®. Copyright © 1973, 1978, 1984 by the International Bible Society. Used by permission of Zondervan Publishing House. All rights reserved.

The "NIV" and "New International Version" trademarks are registered in the United States Patent and Trademark Office by the International Bible Society. Use of either trademark requires the permission of the International Bible Society.

Verses marked "TLB" are taken from THE LIVING BIBLE, © 1971 by Tyndale House Publishers, Wheaton, IL. Used by permission.

Copyright © 1994 Concordia Publishing House
3558 S. Jefferson Avenue, St. Louis, MO 63118-3968
Manufactured in the United States of America

All rights reserved. No part of this publication may be reproduced, stored in a retrieval system, or transmitted, in any form or by any means, electronic, mechanical, photocopying, recording, or otherwise, without the prior written permission of Concordia Publishing House.

1 2 3 4 5 6 7 8 9 10   03 02 01 00 99 98 97 96 95 94

Contents

1 The Junk-Food Finders   5

2 Secret Soup   17

3 Silly Salad   27

4 The VBS Campout   41

5 Pancake Sundae   53

The Junk-Food Finders

Luke threw his backpack on the kitchen table. "Mom, I'm home from school," he yelled.

"Hi, honey," his mother called. "I'm finishing a report on the computer."

Luke grabbed a handful of chips from the bag in the pantry. Then he popped open a can of cherry soda. Bubbles danced on his upper lip as he took a long, hard gulp.

He said hi to his mom in the den. Then Luke settled down on the sofa in the family room. "Hi, Cocoa," he called. The pet hamster stuck his little nose through the cage and sniffed. "Sorry, boy, chips and soda aren't good for you. Laura says we can only feed you hamster pellets."

Just then his sister ran in the front door. "Hi, Luke. Hi, Cocoa," said Laura. "Guess what?"

"You and Martha Louise are best friends again, right?"

Laura stuck out her tongue. "You're mean," she said, frowning. "You always make fun of us. You're crabby too."

Luke knew his sister was right. He did pick on her too much. Mother had told him to let her be. But it was hard. Sometimes she did the dumbest things. If only she would listen to him. He was in fourth grade. Fourth graders know more than first grade kids.

Luke yawned. He felt sleepy. Maybe a couple of cookies would wake him up. He walked into the kitchen to the cookie jar. Just as he reached in, he felt Laura tugging at his sleeve. "Laura to Luke. Laura to Luke," she said laughing. "Anybody home?"

Luke could feel his face get hot. Laura was teasing him. He teased her in the same way when she stared out the window. Or when she was thinking and not listening. This time she caught him.

"Yes, I'm home," he said in a loud voice. "What do you want?"

"I'm going to be a junk-food finder," said Laura. Then she pulled out a pink paper from her Snow-White lunch box. "Look," she said. "We're learning about junk food—the kind with too much sugar and salt and fat—like cupcakes and donuts and salty chips and . . . ."

Luke could see Laura staring at the double fudge chocolate cookie in his hand. He pushed her away. "I don't want to hear about junk food," he said. Then he bit into the cookie and poured another glass of cherry soda.

Luke saw tears come into Laura's eyes. And her mouth turned down. He knew he had hurt her feelings. I'll be in big trouble if Dad finds out, thought Luke.

"Okay, Laura, I'm sorry. Calm down, all right? Tell me about it."

Laura sniffed and wiped her nose with her sleeve. "Are you sure? You're not just saying that?"

"Honest" said Luke. He tried real hard to listen even though all this talk about food made him even more hungry. He loved cupcakes and donuts and soda and chips.

"Some foods are good for our bodies," said Laura, smiling again. "Like fruit and salad and whole wheat bread and brown rice and . . . " Laura's voice trailed off. "Luke, you're not listening to me."

Luke sat up straight. He tried to listen, but it was so boring. Who wants to talk about salad and rice, thought Luke. I'd rather talk about ice cream with hot fudge sauce on top.

"Remember when I told you not to feed Cocoa people food?" asked Laura. "Well," she said, twirling her ponytail, "People should only eat what's good for them too."

Laura took a deep breath. "Luke, did you know that ice cream has so much fat and sugar it can make you sick? Mrs. Kovack said plain yogurt with fresh fruit and nuts would be much better. And it tastes good too. We had some for our snack."

Laura curled up on the carpet under the window. "Good food gives us energy to work and play. See Luke?" Laura held up a drawing of children on swings and slides. "Junk food can make us sleepy and cranky." Another picture showed two kids lying on the floor watching TV and two other kids fighting.

Laura jumped up and smoothed her blue tights. "But that's not for me," she said. "I'm going to be a junk-food finder."

Luke stuffed his mouth with the last bite of cookie and gulped down his soda. Oh great! he thought. Now she's going to bug Mom and Dad. If they believe Laura, we'll turn into health nuts like the Wongs. Their kids take vegetables and bean dip to school. Yuk!

"Did you know it's good to drink six glasses of water everyday?" asked Laura. She flipped her ponytail with her hand. And she pushed up the sleeves of her Beauty-and-the-Beast sweatshirt. "It's hot in here. I think I'll drink some water right now."

"Have some soda," said Luke. "There's one more can of cherry in the 'fridge."

"No thanks," said Laura. "I don't like those little bubbles. They give me a tummy ache. Besides, Mrs. Kovack said that water is better for you. Drinking water is like washing yourself on the inside. Isn't that neat? When you take a bath, you clean the outside of your body. And when you drink water, you clean the inside!" Laura broke into a big smile. "Water is vital to life," she added. Then she took a long drink from the cooler.

"*Vital?*" Luke repeated the word in a high-pitched voice. "Is that one of your *new* words?" he asked.

"Yes it is," Laura snapped. "Vital means *very important*. Water is so important that if we didn't have it we would die."

Luke didn't know what to say. Laura was always surprising him with new words. "Laura, you thought it was fun getting a dictionary for your birthday. That's weird."

Laura's mouth turned down again.

"Just kidding," Luke said. He knew he was heading for trouble if he kept bugging her.

"Let me see that paper," said Luke, taking it from Laura's hand. Maybe first grade kids aren't so dumb after all, he thought. He read the words out loud.

JOIN THE JUNK-FOOD FINDERS

Dear Moms and Dads, and Brothers and Sisters:

We have a new club in our class. It's called the Junk-Food Finders. We're learning about different kinds of food. Food that gives us energy is called health food. Fresh fruit, vegetables, salads, natural cereal, and whole wheat bread are some health foods. Food that takes away our energy is called junk food. Junk food has too much fat and sugar and salt. Greasy donuts, fizzy soda, salty chips, ice cream, and some cookies and cake are junk food. They can make us sleepy and lazy and even sick.

Please help us:

1. Find the junk food in our house and get rid of it.
2. Eat fresh fruit and vegetables every day.
3. Drink four to six glasses of water each day.
4. Eat whole grain bread and cereal each day.
5. Eat fewer foods with fat and sugar.

Come to our Food Fair Monday night at 6:30. Please bring one healthy food and one junk food for Show and Tell. Thank you for helping us.

Mrs. Kovack's First Grade Class

Luke put the paper on the kitchen table. Wait till Mom reads this, he thought. That will be the last of the chips and dips and cherry soda. And I bet she'll never buy double-fudge chocolate cookies again either.

"I think this is a dumb idea," said Luke. He knew his voice sounded mean, but he didn't care. No little kid was going to tell him how to eat. "I don't want to join your silly club," he said. "I bet Mom and Dad won't join either. We like our food just fine. You're the only one in our family who likes weird stuff," said Luke.

Laura burst into tears. Just then Mom walked into the family room. I'm in trouble now, thought Luke.

"Why, Laura, honey, what's wrong? Are you hurt?" She put her arm around Laura and pulled her onto her lap on the sofa.

Luke felt sick inside. He'd have to tell his mother the truth.

She looked at him as if she could see straight through to the other side. "Luke, you don't look well either," she said. "What is going on, you two?" She folded her arms across her chest. "Let's talk about this right now."

Before Laura could say a word, Luke jumped in. He told his mother about the club and how important it is to eat foods without too much fat and sugar and salt.

If I show her how much I know, he thought, maybe she won't be mad at me.

"And, Mom," he said, without stopping for a breath, "did you know everyone should drink water instead of soda? Water cleans you inside just like taking a bath cleans you outside."

"What a good way to explain it," said Mother. "Where did you learn that?"

Luke noticed that Laura's tears were gone and she was smiling—right at him.

"Laura told me," Luke said softly. "She knows more about what's good for our bodies than anybody else."

"Gosh, Luke, thanks. You said everything just right." Laura giggled. "You sound like a junk-food finder already and you didn't even join the club yet."

Luke took a deep breath. He felt as small as an ant. He didn't really care about anything he said. He knew he had talked fast so his mother wouldn't ask any questions. But Laura believed him. She was smiling again.

"I-I-I . . . " The words got stuck in his throat. I've got to say something nice, he thought. I've got to. "I'm, I'm . . . " The words stuck again. "I think the junk-food-finders club is a great idea," he said. "I'll help you." There. He said something nice. Luke took another deep breath.

Now Mother was smiling at him too. Luke felt like an ant again. His mother and his sister thought he was being nice. But inside Luke knew the truth. He hated the whole idea of being a junk-food finder.

Mother read the pink paper out loud. "I believe we have some work ahead of us," she said. "I think this calls for a family meeting. We want Daddy to be in on this too."

"Really?" Luke felt his stomach flip-flop.

"Yeah," shouted Laura. "We can all be junk-food finders."

This was not going the way Luke hoped it would. Now Dad will help too, he thought. There goes my double-fudge cookies for sure. I'll probably never taste one again for the rest of my life. It's not fair.

"Do you know anyone who can help me clean out the pantry?" Mother teased. "Someone who knows the difference between junk food and healthy food?"

"I do," shouted Laura. "Do you want to help me, Luke?"

"Okay," Luke said out loud. But in his mind he was thinking, no way!

"Good. Let's get started," said Mother. First we'll look in the pantry, next the 'fridge, and then the freezer. I've wanted to do this for a long time." Luke watched his mother tie an apron around her waist. It was the pretty flowered one he gave her for Mother's Day.

13

"Mrs. Wong believes something I eat causes my headaches," said Mother. "Too much sugar," she said. "I admit I've been lazy about it."

Mom? Lazy? Luke couldn't imagine his mother being lazy. Grandma called her a tornado because she whirled through the house doing one job after another.

"Afterwards we'll go to the store and buy healthy food and lots of fresh fruit and vegetables," Mother continued. "Maybe we can even find some cookies that don't have fat or sugar. And on the way home I'll buy that book Mrs. Wong told me about. I think it's called, *Raising Healthy Children*."

Luke sunk deeper into the sofa as Mother rolled up her sleeves and walked over to the pantry. He could already see his new school lunches—vegetables and bean dip, just like the Wongs.

"Look at all these chips and crackers and cookies," Mother said as she pulled out some half-empty boxes and bags. She sighed. "I think it's time we stopped talking about eating healthy and did something about it," she said. "We need to show it by our actions."

Show it by our actions. Luke could feel his heart pounding. Where had he heard those words before? At vacation Bible school, that's where. He even memorized a Bible verse about it. It's on the bulletin board, he remembered.

Luke walked into the kitchen and pulled a small paper off the bulletin board. "Little children, let us stop just *saying* we love people; let us *really* love them, and *show* it by our *actions*" (1 John 3:18 TLB). The words *show it by our actions* were highlighted with a yellow marking pen. Luke remembered his teacher telling the boys and girls that their actions were more important than their words. She said, "Remember Jesus' actions, especially His most loving one—giving His life for us on the cross. He will help you love other people.

Luke read the verse two times. He could ask Jesus to forgive him for being mean and selfish. Laura was his sister. He really did love her. He could learn from her too. That was hard to admit, but he knew it was true. Luke walked back into the family room, just as Mother picked up her car keys. She put a cover over Cocoa's cage and then told Luke and Laura to get into the car.

Luke knew he couldn't change all at once. But he could start.

As Laura skipped past him, Luke reached out and grabbed her hand. "Here come The Junk-Food Finders!" he shouted as they ran out the front door. And he really meant it.

BE A JUNK-FOOD FINDER

Talk to your mom and dad and brothers and sisters about what you learned in this story. Ask your parents to help you start a junk-food-finders club in your house. Ask your teacher to start one in school.

Make a poster to help you remember some things to do each day:

1. Find the junk food in our house and get rid of it.
2. Eat fresh fruit and vegetables every day.
3. Drink four to six glasses of water each day.
4. Eat whole grain bread and cereal each day.
5. Eat fewer foods with fat and sugar.

Secret Soup

Luke pulled a cookbook off the shelf over the kitchen counter. He paged through it quickly. Then he read some of the recipes out loud. "Summer squash with cherry tomatoes and capers." What are capers, Luke wondered. He was sure it was something kids wouldn't like.

Luke continued reading. "Asparagus spears with lime dill dressing." No way, he thought.

"Gosh, this is harder than I thought it would be," he said. "I shouldn't have waited so long."

Luke's dad walked into the kitchen. He pulled a sweatshirt over his head. "I'm going jogging before dinner," he said. "Sounds as if you've got a problem. Can I help?"

"No," said Luke in a low voice. "It's too late. We're having a spring vegetable fair at school tomorrow. I wanted to enter the cooking contest. Mr. Bartelli says

boys can cook just as good as girls. But I can't find a vegetable recipe I can make by myself."

"That does sound like a problem," said Dad. "I'm not much good in the veggie department," he added, laughing. "Spaghetti with marinara and mushrooms is my specialty, remember?" Dad winked, grabbed a cap from the hook by the door, and waved good-bye. "Ask Mom," he called from the doorway. "I'll bet she'll have an idea for you."

I wish I *could* ask Mom, Luke thought. But she and Laura are at Grandma's and won't be home till dinner. It'll be too late then, for sure.

Luke felt his stomach churn. He knew he shouldn't have waited until the night before the contest. He was always late. Luke wished he could break this bad habit.

He put away the cookbook and walked out to the backyard. "Hi, there, little buddy," called Mr. Hin over the fence. "You don't look too happy."

"I'm not. I'm mad," said Luke. He looked at the ground and folded his arms across his chest.

Mr. Hin rested his garden hoe against the fence. "Do you want someone to talk to?" he asked softly. "I'm a good listener," he said.

"I don't feel much like talking," said Luke. But then suddenly he spilled out the whole story. He told his neighbor about the vegetable fair and how long he had waited to find a recipe for the contest.

"You're in quite a stew," said Mr. Hin.

A stew? Luke tried not to giggle out loud. I wonder if it's vegetable stew, he thought. Mr. Hin sure loves vegetables. Look at that garden. Bright red cherry tomatoes grew next to the house. Tall corn plants stood against the back fence. Fluffy green carrot tops poked above the ground. And heads of lettuce were lined up behind rows of pea pods.

"Do you think I could have a garden like that someday?" Luke asked.

"I don't see why not," said Mr. Hin. "It's easier than you think. It's fun too. And there's nothing quite like the taste of homegrown vegetables," he added, smacking his lips.

Mr. Hin took off his straw hat and wiped his face with a blue and white handkerchief. "I get mighty hot working out here," he said. "Time for a tall glass of fresh carrot juice," he said. Mr. Hin picked a bunch of carrots from his garden. "Care to join me, Luke?"

Carrot juice? Luke had tasted apple and cranberry and grape juices. But he'd never even heard of carrot juice.

"I-I guess so," he said.

Luke hopped the fence and followed Mr. Hin into the little kitchen. "Mmmm, something smells good," said Luke. "What is it?"

"Vegetable stew," said Mr. Hin.

Luke covered his mouth. He laughed to himself. Vegetable stew. I was right, he thought.

After Mr. Hin washed the carrots, he turned on his juice machine and stuffed the carrots in one by one. Then he and Luke sat down at the table in the corner and sipped their juice. "This tastes good," said Luke.

"And it's good for you," said Mr. Hin. "Excuse me while I check my stew."

Luke watched as Mr. Hin stirred the pot of vegetables. It smelled so-o-o good. Luke remembered that just a few weeks before he hardly knew what a vegetable looked like. He only ate one bite each night because his mother wouldn't let him leave the table unless he did.

Now he actually liked the taste of a whole bunch of vegetables—corn and beets, and peas and carrots. Even carrot juice! And he liked chard. It was dark green and looked like lettuce. It sure tasted good sauteed with garlic and onion and tomatoes and mushrooms. Mr. Bartelli had introduced the kids in the Junior Chef Club to so many new healthy foods. Luke laughed. He even knew the meaning of the French word *saute*. It means to cook in a little oil on high heat, Luke thought to himself. I bet Laura doesn't know *that* word.

Luke glanced at the clock above the stove. "Wow! Five o'clock. I've got to go," he said. "Mom wants me to have the table set for dinner by 5:30. And I haven't even done my homework yet."

Mr. Hin patted Luke on the head. "Run along, little buddy." Then he grabbed Luke by the arm. "Hold on a minute. Why don't you pick a few vegetables from my garden? Your mother might like to make up a pot of soup or a salad. You can surprise her. Here, use my basket. You can bring it back tomorrow."

Luke grabbed the basket and walked toward the door. "And Luke," Mr. Hin said with a twinkle in his eye, "remember, the secret of good vegetable soup is a little bit of this and a little bit of that from God's green earth. Put it all together and you'll have a dish fit for a king."

"Hey, thanks, Mr. Hin."

Luke dashed out to the yard. He grabbed a handful of carrots, some pea pods, two large, ripe tomatoes, and a couple of onions. He carried them home in the basket.

Luke washed his hands, then set the placemats on the kitchen table. He put out the plates and silverware and napkins and glasses.

Just then Luke's dad jogged in the back door. He tossed his cap on the counter and pulled off his sweatshirt. "Hey, you've been busy, Luke. Thanks for setting the table. What's for dinner? Are you the cook?"

Luke knew his dad was trying to cheer him up, but nothing could help now. It was too late for him to enter the contest. He was so mad he didn't even feel like eating dinner.

Luke's dad stroked his chin. Luke could tell he was thinking about something important. "Luke, while I was jogging I got an idea," he said. "Why don't you make something easy—you know—something you can do without a recipe. Even if you don't win the contest, at least you'll have tried."

Dad leaned his forehead against Luke's forehead. "Why don't we put our heads together on this one?" he asked, laughing.

Luke laughed too. I have the best dad in the whole world, he thought.

"I'm going to take a quick shower," said Dad. "Then we'll see what we can come up with."

Luke walked over to the sink. He looked at the basket of vegetables from Mr. Hin's garden. "A little bit of this and a little bit of that from God's green earth," he mumbled, remembering what his neighbor had said.

"Hey, that's it," Luke shouted. "Vegetable soup. I can stick a whole bunch of vegetables in Mom's big pot, fill it up with water, add some garlic and onion powder and maybe some salt and pepper and...."

Luke pulled out the big soup pot and half-filled it with water. Then he took the vegetables out of Mr. Hin's basket and rinsed them under cool water. He'd seen Mom do that a whole bunch of times before.

He knew he shouldn't turn on the stove without an adult watching. And Dad didn't want him using the big knife without help. Okay. He'd wait till Dad finished his shower. "This is going to be fun—and delicious," he said out loud.

A few minutes later Dad walked into the kitchen, smelling all clean. "All right," he said, as he tied an apron around his waist. "Let's get to work. The grill sergeant has arrived."

Luke laughed. "Dad, I need help with the stove and the knife, but that's all. I got a great idea while you were in the shower."

Then Luke told Dad about his visit with Mr. Hin. He told him about the garden and the carrot juice and the vegetable stew. "And he let me pick these vegetables out of his garden," said Luke. "I'm going to make soup."

"What kind?" asked Dad. "I don't know what it's called," said Luke. "It's going to have a little bit of this and a little bit of that."

"Sounds like a secret to me," said Dad.

"Hey, maybe I could call it *Secret Soup*," said Luke in his most important voice. "Even if I don't win, at least I tried."

Luke peeled the carrots, pulled the peas out of their shells, chopped up the onions as Dad watched, and cut up the tomatoes. He found two small potatoes in the vegetable bin, some fresh mushrooms in the refrigerator, and a little sprig of parsley in Mom's window garden.

Luke added some garlic powder, vegetable seasoning from the pantry, and a dash of salt and pepper. He turned on the stove, and with Dad's help, he stirred the mixture until it started to bubble. Then he turned the heat to low, covered the pot, and set the timer for one hour.

At 6:30, Luke heard Mother's car drive into the garage. Won't she be surprised, thought Luke. I made Secret Soup all by myself, with a little bit of this and a little bit of that.

Dad lifted the cover on the pot and sniffed the boiling soup. "I wish we could eat some right now," he said. "I'm starved, and I'll bet Mom and Laura are hungry too. I could make some garlic toast to go with it and we could have Mrs. Wong's walnut cookies for dessert."

Luke was so excited he thought his heart would burst. "That's a great idea, Dad. Sounds like a meal fit for a king."

Dad ruffled Luke's hair. Then Luke ran out to meet Mom and Laura. "Hurry up," he called. "Soup's on and I made it all by myself."

Make Your Own Secret Soup

(With a Little Bit of This and a Little Bit of That)

Ask a parent or another adult to help you. Start with this simple recipe for vegetable soup. Use other vegetables if you want. Add mushrooms or peas or corn to create your very own secret soup. No one will know the recipe except you and your helper! Serve your secret soup to your family and friends.

Easy-to-make Vegetable Soup

Here is what you need:

- 2 tablespoons of safflower oil
- 1 yellow onion, cut in thin half-circles
- 3 large stalks of celery, sliced
- 2 large carrots, sliced
- 1 zucchini squash, sliced
- 2 medium red potatoes, cut in cubes
- 3 cups of thinly sliced green cabbage
- 8 cups of water
  Vegetable seasoning or salt and pepper to taste

Here's what to do:

1. Put water, seasonings, and oil in a large pot.
2. Add the vegetables.
3. Cook on high until the soup comes to a boil.
4. Turn to low and cook for one hour.
5. Serve with warm whole-wheat bread or whole grain rolls.

Silly Salad

Luke ran down the stairs two at a time. He grabbed his baseball mitt from the hall closet. "See you later, Mom," he called and ran out the front door.

"Hold on, young man!" she shouted. Luke spun around. Mom stood on the front step with her hands on her hips. "Aren't you forgetting something?"

"Oh, my cap." Luke dashed back into the house and grabbed his baseball cap off the hat rack. "Thanks, Mom," he said and kissed her on the cheek.

Mom snatched Luke's hat and wagged it in front of him. "Not your hat, Luke. I'm talking about my luncheon at church," she said. "You promised to make pasta salad, remember?"

"And I'm going to make Raisin-Walnut Rice Pudding," Laura called out the front door.

Mother turned to Laura. "The rice is all cooked," she said. "Just mix in the maple syrup and the milk the

way I showed you and stir in a few walnuts and raisins. Mr. Hin said he'll help you heat it up."

Luke punched his fist into his mitt. Now he remembered. Mom had told him last night that she and Dad had to finish a tax report by noon. The luncheon would start at 12:30. She wouldn't have time to fix the food, get dressed, and drive to church in so little time. She needed their help.

Mother's voice broke into Luke's thoughts. "You kids said you'd fix the food if I put out the recipes." Mother took a deep breath and frowned at Luke. "I'll have to hurry as it is."

Luke felt as small as an ant. It seemed he was always forgetting something important. Boy! Kevin sure will be mad, thought Luke. I promised him we could practice pitching and catching all morning.

Mother put her arms around Luke and kissed his head. "I know you're disappointed, Luke," she said softly. "But I can't let you run out on me this way. I'm counting on you."

"But Mom . . . " Luke knew it wouldn't do any good to argue. He just hoped his friend would understand. Luke walked into the house slowly, picked up the phone in the kitchen, and dialed Kevin's number. He explained the problem. Kevin didn't sound happy, but he wasn't real mad either.

Luke washed his hands in the kitchen sink. Mother walked in carrying a huge wooden bowl and two pieces of paper. "Here's your recipe for the salad," she said, handing Luke a green paper. "The curly-cue pasta is cooked and in the 'fridge. Everything else is there too."

Mother picked up her car keys and headed for the door. "Oh, Luke," she called, and turned around. "I almost forgot. Laura is going to help Mr. Hin plant some marigolds. He said he'd look out for the two of you. We won't be gone long. If you need anything, ask Mr. Hin. He'll be working in his flower garden all morning."

Mother blew Luke a kiss. "When Laura is done helping, please ask her to decorate the bowl of pudding with some carob chips. Tell her to make it real pretty." She pointed to the pantry. "They're in a little bag on the second shelf. The walnuts and raisins are there too. Bye, honey, and thanks again. You're a good sport. I love you."

"I love you too, Mom," Luke mumbled. He didn't feel like a good sport. He was almost sorry he had joined the Junior Chef Club at school. Now Mom thought he could cook practically anything. Luke picked up the paper with the recipe on it and looked at the list.

Then he sat down next to Cocoa's cage and waved the paper in front of the hamster. "I like to cook," he said, "but not as much as I like to play baseball. You're lucky, Cocoa. You get to play all day and somebody feeds you too." Luke opened the door and reached in to pet the hamster. But Cocoa didn't wait to be petted. He dashed out of the cage and raced across the room.

"Cocoa, come back. Come back. Mom'll really be mad now. If you get away, I'm in big trouble." Luke chased the hamster all over the kitchen and family room. Cocoa raced around the television. Then he squeezed under the sofa. But when Luke tried to grab him, he dashed across the carpet into the kitchen. Luke was nearly out of breath. "Cocoa, you bad little hamster. Get over here right now."

Cocoa did not obey. Luke could tell he was having fun. He liked running all over the room. I bet he's sick of that exercise wheel, Luke thought. He reached out one more time but Cocoa was too fast. The little hamster crept around the side of the pantry and squeezed behind the refrigerator. Then Luke saw two shiny eyes peer around the side of the 'fridge.

"Here, Cocoa. Here, Cocoa," Luke called. He grabbed a carrot top and waved it in front of the hamster. Cocoa ran toward the greens and Luke backed up toward the cage. "That's my boy," he said. "Keep coming. You can have the carrot top but you have to get back in your cage first."

Luke bent down slowly and quietly. He laid the carrot greens inside the cage and pushed the door wide open. Cocoa stopped. His little eyes darted back and forth.

"I know you're scared," said Luke. "It's all right," he coaxed softly. "This is your home. I can't let you run around like this. I'm counting on you to get back in your cage right now."

Suddenly Luke's heart started pounding fast. Hadn't his mother said almost the same thing to him just a couple of hours ago? "I can't let you run out on me," she had said. "I'm counting on you."

Just then Cocoa ran past Luke. He stopped in front of his cage and picked up a little piece of colored paper with his teeth. Then he ran inside. Luke slammed the door closed and locked it. "Whew! That was close," he said. Luke laughed as he watched Cocoa chewing the paper. "He thinks it's food," he laughed.

Suddenly Luke realized what Cocoa was eating. He felt a big pain in his stomach. "Oh my gosh," he groaned. "That's the paper with the recipe for the salad. Now what'll I do?"

Luke glanced at the clock on the oven and his stomach hurt even more. "Eleven-thirty! Mom'll be home at 12," he said out loud. "I only have a half hour to make the salad." Luke looked at Cocoa and yelled as loud as he could. "It's your fault, you stupid hamster. You ruined everything."

Luke waved his arms around and stamped his feet. The little hamster curled up in the corner of his cage. Luke could see Cocoa was afraid. But he didn't care. He kept right on screaming.

"Why couldn't you stay in your cage where you belong? And why did you have to eat the recipe? Don't you know the difference between a carrot top and a piece of paper?"

Luke flopped down on the floor. Tears rolled down his cheeks. Everything was going wrong this morning. His Saturday was ruined. Maybe even his whole life! He couldn't play catch with Kevin. Mom needed him to cook when he'd rather be out playing. And then Cocoa ate the recipe.

"God, you said you'd never leave me," Luke prayed out loud. "Remember when Miss Hanley taught us that Bible verse in vacation Bible school? Well, God, it sure feels like you left me. How am I going to make the salad when I don't have the recipe? And even if I did have it, there isn't enough time."

Luke dried his eyes with his shirt sleeve and stood up. "Mom was counting on me and I goofed. I counted on Cocoa to behave and he ran away. Lord, now I'm counting on you. I sure hope what Miss Hanley said is true. Amen."

Luke walked over to the refrigerator and poured a glass of lemonade. He remembered when he used to drink cherry soda and eat double-fudge cookies. Now the 'fridge was filled with good, healthy food like lemonade and tomatoes and carrots and raisins and nuts.

"Hey, wait a minute. I remember Mom saying that everything I need for the salad is right here. I don't know how much I should put in the bowl but maybe I could use a little bit of this and a little bit of that. That's what I did for my Secret Soup and everybody thought it was great."

Luke tied his Junior Chef apron around his waist. And he smiled for the first time all morning. "I've got to try, Lord," he prayed. "Mom's counting on me."

Luke opened the refrigerator and pulled out a small bunch of carrots, the pasta curly cues, a ripe tomato, a small brown onion, and a yellow pepper.

Then he opened the pantry and took out the garlic and vegetable seasoning. He had seen Mother sprinkle this on all their food. "It's healthier than salt," she had said. And he grabbed a new bottle of lime dill salad dressing.

Luke was just about to close the pantry door when he noticed a small bag on the second shelf. "Carob chips. I almost forgot," he said. "And here's a little box of raisins and some walnuts."

Luke felt proud. It was all coming back to him. He remembered that Mom had said something about carob chips and raisins and walnuts. No problem, Luke thought. "This'll be easy. I'll just throw everything into the bowl and pour a little dressing on it," he said to himself.

Laura pushed open the door and stepped inside. She was wearing garden gloves that were too big for her and her sunhat fell over her right eye. "Hi, Luke," she said. "Are you finished with the salad yet? Mom said we should take turns in the kitchen so we don't fight."

"Almost finished," Luke said proudly. "I'll call you in about five minutes."

"Okay," said Laura. She put a yellow and a purple tulip in the vase on the kitchen table. Then she filled it with fresh water.

"I'll help Mr. Hin clean up before lunch," she said. "Then I'll fix the pudding."

"Sure, Laura, sure," Luke mumbled. He didn't want to talk about her pudding now. He had work to do.

Luke took out the salad shooter. It was easy for a kid to use. It worked with a battery. Luke put in the peeled carrots, the onion, and the pepper. The vegetable pieces zoomed out the end and into the wooden bowl. "This is fun," said Luke. "Mom will be so proud of me." Then he added the cherry tomatoes.

Luke picked up the big salad fork and spoon and mixed the vegetable slices and tomatoes with the curly pasta. Then he opened the bag of carob chips. "I think I'll use all of them," he said. "There'll be a lot of ladies at the luncheon." Next he crushed three walnuts in his hand and dropped them into the bowl. And last, he sprinkled some raisins into the salad and mixed everything together with the lime dill dressing.

"I wish I could go to the church luncheon," said Luke. "This salad looks so good I could eat the whole bowl myself."

Luke covered the salad and shoved it into the refrigerator. He put the dirty dishes and spoons in the dishwasher. Then he wiped the counter with a wet sponge.

"You can have the kitchen now," he called to Laura from the back door.

Luke sat down at the kitchen table. He turned the pages of a baseball magazine while Laura fixed the pudding. She added the syrup. Then she opened the pantry. "Hey, Luke, where's the little box of raisins and the walnuts?"

"I don't know, I-I . . . " Luke froze. He dropped the magazine on the table. "Raisins?" he asked. "Walnuts?" He could hear his voice squeak. "I don't know. I mean . . . "

36

Suddenly Luke remembered everything his mother had said. The raisins and walnuts and carob chips were for Laura's pudding, not for his salad.

Luke felt that pain in his stomach again. "Laura, I did a terrible thing. I-I-I put the raisins and the walnuts and the carob chips in the salad. Look!" he said and pulled out the wooden bowl from the refrigerator.

Laura burst out laughing. "Luke, that is the silliest looking salad I ever saw."

"Yeah, but Laura, it tastes good." Luke could feel his hands turn sweaty he was so nervous. "Want to try some?" Luke gave his sister a spoonful.

"Yum!" she said.

Just then Mother walked through the front door. "Dad had to run an errand," she said. "He'll meet me at the church. Well, my little chefs," she said smiling. "Are the salad and pudding ready to go?"

Luke took a big gulp of air. "Sort of. Mom, I can explain. Please don't be mad. You see, Cocoa got loose and I-I . . ." Luke almost told a lie. Then he remembered that he had asked God to help him.

Laura jumped in. "Mom, wait till you see what Luke did. He made a new kind of salad. It has walnuts and raisins and carob chips. I mean they're kind of silly for a salad, don't you think?" Laura hopped up and down on one foot.

"But, Mom," she said, almost out of breath, "it tastes great. Want to try some?"

"Not now, dear. Sounds like you have a story to tell me, Luke," she said. "I want to hear all about it, especially the part about Cocoa and the carob chips and the raisins." Mother raised her eyebrows, but Luke could tell she wasn't mad. "We'll have to wait till I get back. I'm in a hurry now. Allison will be along to babysit in a few minutes." Mother ruffled Luke's hair and ran upstairs.

"Gee, thanks, Laura," said Luke. "You saved my neck. But what about the pudding? You didn't get to decorate it with carob chips and it's all my fault."

"It's okay, Luke. I put chopped dates on top. They look real pretty."

"You're not only my sister, Laura. You're a good friend," said Luke.

Just then Mother popped her head around the corner. "Luke," she said, "will you please tape this sign to the side of the bowl and, Laura, put this one on the bowl of pudding. I want everyone to know who deserves the credit for these delicious foods."

Luke looked at his sign: "Silly Salad by Junior Chef Luke Taylor." Luke smiled. He watched Laura tape her sign to the bowl of pudding: "Laura Taylor's Special Pudding."

Luke hugged Mother good-bye. Then he closed his eyes for a minute. "Lord, *You* deserve the credit," Luke prayed quietly. "Thanks for staying with me. Miss Hanley was right."

MAKE YOUR OWN SILLY SALAD

You can make your own silly salad. Start with cooked pasta. Then from the list below, pick three vegetables and two extras. Mix them together in a big bowl. Toss lightly with your favorite salad dressing. Serve on a lettuce leaf.

Cooked pasta
(Read the package for cooking directions.)

Pasta comes in many different shapes such as curly cues, wagon wheels, bow ties, and others. Some come in a mix of colors too. Look in a health food store or grocery store.

Vegetables (1 cup)
Carrot slices
Cherry tomatoes, cut in half
Chopped zucchini
Broccoli florets
   (the flower part of the vegetable)
Sliced water chestnuts

Extras (1/8 cup)
Raw sunflower or pumpkin seeds
   (find in health food store)
Raisins
Carob chips
Chopped walnuts
Black olive slices

4

The VBS Campout

"Hey, Miss Hanley, Miss Hanley!" Luke ran to the front of the church hall. Vacation Bible school is over next Friday, right?"

"Right," she said, smiling. "The first week went fast, didn't it, Luke?"

"Yeah. Only one week to go. Are we going to have a party—you know, like a good-bye party or something?" Luke could feel his heart pounding. He shifted from one foot to the other as he talked.

"Why, yes we are. Kevin's father is bringing punch and Gretchen's mother offered to bake cookies. How does that sound?"

"Okay, I guess." Luke sighed and looked at the ground. He kicked a piece of paper with his shoe.

Then he felt Miss Hanley's hand on his shoulder. "Luke, is there something wrong?"

"Not wrong, exactly. But punch and cookies doesn't sound like a fun party to me. We always have

41

that. It's not special." Luke looked up. Miss Hanley was smiling. He could feel his courage building. "I was thinking we could have a really neat party. The kind we would always remember."

"What did you have in mind?" asked Miss Hanley.

Luke looked at the students' paintings on the wall. All week they had studied about God's earth in VBS. They read the story of creation from the Bible. And they painted a mural showing all the things God had made. They sang songs and took nature walks. They even planted flowers and bushes around the church yard.

"We studied about God's earth all week," said Luke. "So I wish we could have a nature party, something outdoors. Like a campout," he added. "We could even have a campfire and pop popcorn. We could sing worship songs and look at the stars and . . . " Luke felt excited just thinking about a VBS campout.

"It's a wonderful idea," said Miss Hanley. "But we don't have enough time left to plan such a trip." Then she picked up her books and turned toward Luke. "Let's keep it in mind for next year," she said smiling. Miss Hanley picked up her books and walked toward the front door.

Luke took a deep breath and followed his teacher outside. "It sure is hot," he said. Then he pulled up his yellow t-shirt and wiped his face. He noticed a streak of green paint had dried over the words on his shirt:

Grace Church Vacation Bible School. He hoped it would wash out.

"Punch and cookies. It's not even healthy," Luke muttered to himself.

Miss Hanley turned. "Are you talking to me?" she asked.

Luke felt his face turn warm. "I-I-I was just saying that punch and cookies aren't very healthy." He stumbled over the words.

"My family's learning about natural foods," he said. "I'm a Junior Chef at school and my sister's in a club called The Junk-Food Finders and . . . " The words suddenly tumbled out of Luke's mouth like a waterfall. He told Miss Hanley everything he was learning about eating healthy foods.

"Why, Luke," she said, and turned and walked toward him. "I didn't know that about you."

"I do a lot of cooking at home," said Luke. "My mom's at a conference this week and I'm making dinner almost every night. Dad and Laura help too."

Miss Hanley set her books down on a chair. Then suddenly she clapped her hands together and Luke saw her brown eyes sparkle.

"I have an idea," she said. "How would you like to be in charge of our VBS party? You know more about food than I do! And I like your idea about having the party outdoors—right in God's creation," she said.

Luke felt his face get warm again. "Gee, Miss Hanley, I don't know if I could do the whole party by myself."

"Well, think about it overnight," she said. "I'll ask some of the other students to help you. We can talk more about it tomorrow."

"Okay, Miss Hanley. See you!"

Luke ran out of the church hall and flew down the hill toward his house. He dashed up the driveway and nearly tripped over Laura's bike. "Dad, Laura, guess what?" he shouted as he pushed open the front door.

"We're in the family room," called his father.

"I'm in charge of the VBS party on the last day," said Luke, nearly out of breath from running.

Dad and Laura were changing the newspaper in Cocoa's cage.

"That's quite an honor," said Dad.

Then he told Dad and Laura what he shared with Miss Hanley about healthy eating. "She even said she could learn from me," said Luke proudly, hopping from one foot to another.

"Wow, Luke, you're lucky," said Laura. "Can I help?"

"I don't think so," said Luke in his most important voice. "This is for fourth graders only. Your class will have your own party."

Laura frowned and her lip began to tremble. Luke suddenly felt guilty. If it hadn't been for Laura, he wouldn't even know about healthy foods. And now he was acting like he knew everything and that he didn't need her help.

Luke walked over to Laura. He was too embarrassed to look at her, so he stared at the floor. "Well, maybe you can help me think of what foods we could eat," said Luke.

"Okay. Thanks," said Laura. She smiled again and Luke felt a lot better.

"Do you need help with decorations or posters?" asked Dad, turning toward Luke.

"I'm not sure."

Dad winked. "I'm pretty good with lettering, you know." Then he turned back to Cocoa's cage and finished fitting the paper around the edges.

"I wanted our class to do something outdoors, like camping." Luke took a handful of trail mix from the bowl on the table by the sofa. "Miss Hanley said that's too much work. Maybe next year," he said. Luke picked out two nuts and a couple of raisins and put them on the floor of Cocoa's cage.

"But next year will be too late," he went on. "This is the year we're studying about God's earth and trees and stars and stuff like that. Wouldn't it be neat if on our last day we could, you know, have fun in God's world, not just read about it?"

"Do you mean appreciate it?" asked Laura.

"Yeah. That's right Laura." Luke couldn't believe it. His sister knew so many big words. And she knew what they meant and when to use them. He wished he could think of the right word as fast as she could.

"Well, maybe it's not too late, after all," said Dad. "Let's put our heads together," he said, and leaned his head against Luke's. Laura squeezed between them.

"I want to put my head in too," said Laura.

Dad and Luke laughed. "We can't leave you out, can we?" Dad picked up Laura and bumped heads with her.

"I have an idea," said Dad. "A good game of catch outside will make us feel better. How about it, Luke? You can play too, Laura," he said. "Then we'll talk about the party with Mother when she calls tonight."

"When Mommy comes home, are we going to put four heads together?" asked Laura.

"Not a bad idea," said Dad laughing.

Luke didn't think it was funny. He was worried about the party. He had only a few days to plan the whole thing.

Dad grabbed two mitts from the shelf and Luke ran upstairs to get the ball. Then Dad and Luke and

Laura ran out to the yard and tossed the ball back and forth to each other.

"What kind of parties did you have when you were a kid?" Luke asked, stretching for a catch.

"Our house was in the country so we practically lived outdoors," Dad answered. "In the summertime I don't think I ever slept in my room. Grandma says our tent was my summer home. I even cooked outdoors."

Dad had a far-away look in his eyes. He smiled as he told Luke and Laura some of the fun things he did with his older brother when they were boys.

"What did you like best?" asked Laura.

"That's easy," said Dad. "It was my 10th birthday. I told Grandma I wanted to have a campout with my friends in our yard instead of a party."

Dad stopped playing ball for a minute and plopped on the grass. Luke and Laura sat down next to him. "It's a party I'll always remember," he said. "We did everything real campers do. We cooked our burgers outside and popped popcorn around a campfire."

Dad stretched out on the grass and put his hands under his head. Luke and Laura lay down next to him. Luke noticed that his dad's voice sounded happy every time he talked about the campout.

"We lay on our backs just like we're doing now," he said, "and tried to count the stars. But there were too many to count. We sang worship songs too. My friend

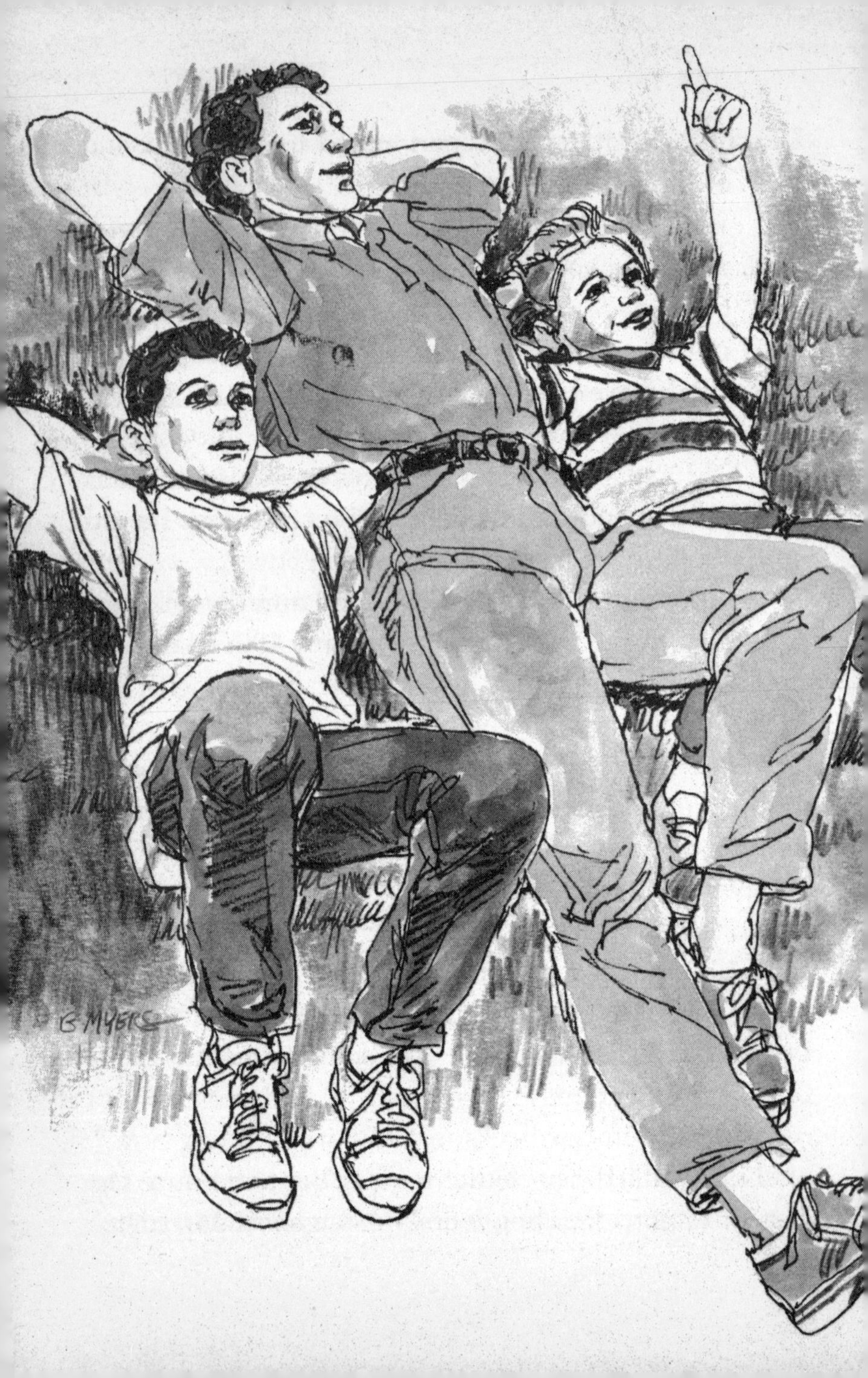

Danny was learning to play the guitar. He wasn't very good, but he knew a couple of songs from church."

Luke tried to imagine what his dad looked like as a little boy. He decided he would look at the pictures of him hanging on the wall in Grandma's house.

"What a great idea for a birthday party," said Luke.

"I want to have a campout in our backyard for my next birthday," said Laura. "Will you help me, Daddy?"

Dad reached out and pulled Laura and Luke in close. "Sure thing," he said. "You can even use my tent. I still have it," he said. "There's room for four people in that old tent."

Luke signed. The good old days sounded like fun. Living in the country and camping and sleeping in a tent. Luke wished his family lived in the country or in the mountains. Then VBS could have a campout every year instead of punch and cookies.

Then suddenly Luke sat up straight. "Hey, wait a minute!" he shouted. "Dad, Laura. I've got an idea for the VBS party. It'll be great for the kids, and it won't be too much work for Miss Hanley."

Dad sat up. Then Laura sat up too. Dad chuckled. "That game of catch really worked, didn't it? Sounds as if you feel better already. What's your idea, Luke?"

"What if we had a campout right here in our yard for the VBS party?" asked Luke. "Four kids could sleep in your tent, Dad. And maybe some other parents have tents too. I know the Wongs do. We only have 12 kids in our class. We could fit them in our yard easy."

"Martha Louise's step-dad has a tent," said Laura. "Maybe you could borrow it."

"Good idea. Thanks, Laura," said Luke.

"What about the food?" asked Dad. "We eat different these days than we used to. I'm not sure how we'd handle that. I'd rather not cook hamburgers."

"You could make veggie burgers," said Laura. "We made some in school and they taste real good with catsup and mustard. Mommy has the recipe."

"Great idea, Laura. And I could make a carrot and raisin salad," said Luke.

"And we could fix a big pitcher of ice water and some fresh-squeezed lemonade." Dad stroked his chin. "And of course popcorn. We can cook the burgers on the outdoor grill and then pop the corn over the fire."

"And for dessert," said Luke, "we'll have apple cobbler."

"Let's get a piece of paper and write all this down," said Dad. "We don't want to forget any of it."

Luke ran into the family room and grabbed the pad of paper and pencil by the phone. Laura found the recipes for the burgers and salad and dessert and handed them to Luke.

Suddenly Luke got a funny feeling in his stomach. "Dad, do you think we can do all this without Mom? A whole party all by ourselves?"

Dad laughed. "Well, it's a tall order, but with an old camper like me around, I think we'll be all right."

Luke took a deep breath. He felt warm all over and happy. He just knew Miss Hanley was going to like the idea. Luke and Laura and Dad would help her do everything.

Everyone would have fun.

They would eat healthy food.

They would be outdoors in God's earth.

And it would be a party everyone would remember—just like Dad's 10th birthday.

Luke picked up his mitt and ball and walked into the house with Dad and Laura. "Thank You, Lord," he whispered, "for Your creation and for my family—and for Dad's old tent."

BACKYARD CAMPOUT

Would you like to have a backyard campout with your family or friends? Set up enough tents for your group. If the night is warm, you may wish to sleep outdoors under the stars.

Each camper will need:
Sleeping bag	Flashlight
Knife, fork, spoon	Dish and cup
Soap and towel	Toothbrush and
Comb and brush	toothpaste
Pajamas	Change of clothes

A game to play:

Squirrel Hunt. Ahead of time, hide peanuts-in-the-shell around the yard. Blow a whistle to start the game. Everyone finds as many peanuts as he or she can. The one with the most wins the game and gets a prize.

A recipe to make:

Food Pouch. Cut a piece of extra-strength aluminum foil large enough to hold a burger and vegetables. Place a vegetable burger (buy in frozen section of a health food store) in the center of the foil. Put four thin slices of cooked potato on top. Then add a small clump of shredded carrot. Sprinkle with salt or garlic seasoning. Add one tablespoon of catsup or barbecue sauce. Close pouch. Fold edges tight. Cook over a hot grill for about 10–15 minutes.

5

Pancake Sundae

Luke looked at the clock over the big iron stove in the Middleberry School kitchen. Five minutes to four. He could hardly wait for the bell to ring.

Mr. Bartelli closed the cookbook in front of him. He looked at the students in the Junior Chef Club. "Good work," he said. "Now you know how to make whole-grain pancakes with fresh fruit topping."

Mr. Bartelli held up a plate of pancakes topped with berries and bananas and syrup. Then he scooped some frozen vanilla yogurt out of a small carton. "Add a little yogurt for an extra treat," he said.

It looks like one of Grandpa's double-decker sundaes, thought Luke. But *this* kind is good for you.

"You could make this for breakfast for your whole family," said Mr. Bartelli.

Luke picked out a blueberry from the bowl of fruit on his work table. He popped it into his mouth. It was

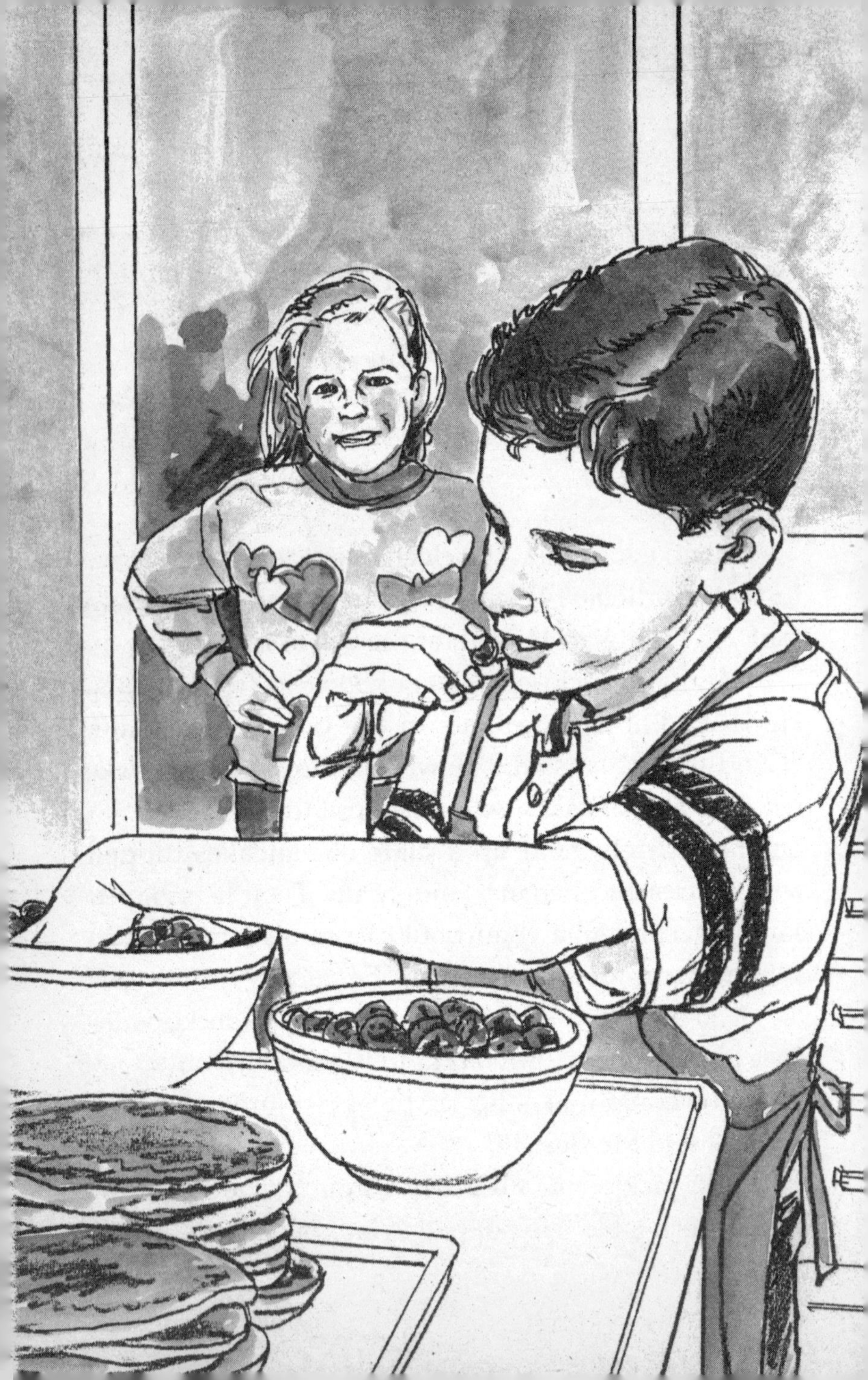

fun making pancakes, but now he was ready to play catch with Kevin.

Just then Luke saw Laura standing by the door. He almost forgot. She had stayed after school to help Mrs. Kovack put up a new bulletin board.

He was supposed to walk home with her.

Mr. Bartelli waved to Laura. "Come in, Laura. We're almost finished. Have a seat next to your brother." Laura squeezed in next to Luke and said hi to everyone at the table.

"Shhh!" Luke said and poked her in the side.

"Boys and girls, just one more thing before you go," said Mr. Bartelli in a loud voice. "We've been talking a lot about how important it is to eat good food—not just good-tasting, but good for you." He pointed to the bulletin board behind his table.

"If you want to help your family learn better eating habits, remember these suggestions." Mr. Bartelli went over each one.

"Number 1. Be kind and patient. Your family may be used to certain foods and may not want to give them up."

"Number 2. Go slowly. Don't expect your parents to clean out the pantry and the refrigerator in one day."

"Our mom did," Laura whispered to Luke.

"Shhh!" Luke said again.

Mr. Bartelli continued.

"Number 3. Make a healthy version of a favorite recipe. For example, if your family eats greasy donuts, offer to make our apple-blueberry bran muffins instead. You could also substitute low-fat yogurt and fresh strawberries for high-fat strawberry ice cream. Look for a way to show your family a healthy alternative."

Luke felt proud. He knew the meaning of the word *alternative*. He didn't have to ask Laura or anyone. He wondered if she knew.

"Luke, did you know an alternative is the same as a choice?" Laura asked. "I heard it on TV and Daddy helped me find it in the big dictionary."

Luke couldn't believe it. This kid is a walking dictionary, he thought.

"And the last one is number 4," Mr. Bartelli continued. "Be a good example. Practice what you are learning. Don't just talk about it."

Mr. Bartelli took off his reading glasses and slipped them into his shirt pocket. "All right. You may go now. Have a happy and healthy weekend. I'll see you after school next Friday."

Luke felt good all over. His mom and dad and sister were eating more healthy foods every day. Everyone felt better. Luke had more energy. His mom didn't have headaches anymore. His dad was jogging again. And Laura didn't wake up at night as much as she used to.

If only Grandpa would change, thought Luke. But he's old. Mr. Bartelli said old people are the hardest ones to change. Luke thought about Grandpa and how much fun it was to play miniature golf with him. They used to stop at the Cold Spot afterwards and share a double-decker banana split sundae.

But not anymore. Luke knew that foods like ice cream have a lot of fat. Too much fat is bad for people. It clogs up their blood vessels and makes it hard for blood to get to the heart. Suddenly Luke felt a little sick in his stomach. I don't want Grandpa to have a heart attack, he worried.

Luke grabbed Laura's hand. They ran out of the cafeteria and all the way home. "Mom, Dad," he called as he pushed open the sliding glass door. "I'm worried about Grandpa," he almost yelled.

Mother looked up from the book she was reading. "Luke, what happened?" she asked.

Dad walked into the family room from the garage. "I heard you calling," he said. "You look as white as paste."

Mother moved to the middle of the sofa and patted the two seats beside her. Luke dropped his books on the rug and sat down. Laura sat down too. "What gave you the idea that Grandpa isn't well?" Mom asked.

Dad sat on the arm rest.

Luke gulped hard before he said anything. "At our Junior Chef Club meeting today we learned about how bad it is to eat foods that have a lot of fat. Mr. Bartelli said ice cream is one of the worst fat foods."

Luke sat up and turned to his mother. "That made me think of Grandpa and all the double-decker sundaes he eats. He's too fat already, Mom. And he keeps eating more ice cream and other junk foods."

"One time I saw him sneaking some candy in the kitchen," said Laura. "He made me promise not to tell Grandma."

Mother's voice was soft. She put her arm around Luke's shoulders and pulled Laura close. "I'm sure Grandpa would feel very special to know you cared about him so much."

"I hope you'll tell him that tomorrow," said Dad.

"Tomorrow?" asked Luke.

"What's tomorrow?" Laura asked.

"We invited Grandpa and Grandma to brunch. It's the first Saturday in a long time when we can all be together," said Mother.

"Can I cook?" asked Luke.

"Daddy and I already have something planned," said Mother, "but thank you for asking."

Luke jumped up from the sofa and paced back and forth. "Mom," he said in a loud voice. "You don't understand. I want to *show* Grandpa that I care about him, not just talk about it. That's one of the rules in our club—be a good example. Practice what you are learning. Don't just talk about it."

"It's number 4," said Laura, smiling. "I heard Mr. Bartelli read it today."

Mother patted Laura's hand. Then she winked at Luke. "Sounds like another chance to put your Bible verse into action," she said.

Luke had almost forgotten. He looked at the verse hanging on the bulletin board. He remembered what his Sunday school teacher had told him about actions being more important than words.

"All right, Luke, the kitchen is yours tomorrow morning." Luke laughed as his father bowed and saluted him. "And just what is his majesty the junior chef going to prepare for this special occasion?"

Luke pulled out the recipe from his pocket. It was pretty wrinkled but he could still read it. "Whole grain pancakes with fresh fruit and low-fat yogurt."

"Sounds wonderful to me," Dad said. "Do you need some help?"

"You could help me with the stove," said Luke. "And Laura, would you make some placemats for the table like you did for Daddy's birthday?"

"Sure, Luke. I'll get my markers and some paper right now."

That night after dinner Mother and Luke cut up fresh fruit. Dad helped Laura make six placemats. She decorated them with pictures of fruit and vegetables. And she wrote one person's name on each placemat.

The next morning Luke got up early. He had a lot of work to do before Grandpa and Grandma arrived. He put on his Junior Chef apron. Then he took out a big bowl and poured in the pancake mix. He cracked an egg on the side of the bowl and added it to the mix. Then he poured in the water and stirred the pancake mix until it was smooth.

Dad turned on the stove and stood nearby as Luke began spooning the mix onto the hot griddle. After all the pancakes were made, Mother put them in a covered dish in the oven to keep them warm.

"Whoops! I almost forgot the most important part," said Luke. "I'll be right back. It's a surprise for Grandpa," said Luke. "You'll see!"

Luke ran up to his room and took out a special card and an envelope. He sat down at his desk, wrote a little note, and signed his name. He put the note in his shirt pocket. Then he raced down the stairs two at a time.

Just then the doorbell rang. Luke ran to the front door and opened it. His tummy flip-flopped, he was so excited. Laura stood beside him.

"Well, what have we got here?" asked Grandpa, tugging at Luke's Junior Chef apron.

Grandpa turned to Grandma and winked. "I believe we're in for a first-class breakfast. We have a real chef in our family."

Grandma scooped Laura into her arms and reached over and kissed Luke on the cheek. "How are my cutie pies?" she asked.

Luke and Laura squirmed and laughed. "We're fine, Grandma," said Luke. "We have a big surprise for you and Grandpa." Luke pulled Grandma and Grandpa into the dining room.

"Sit here and here," said Laura, pointing to the placemats that had their names on them.

Laura and Daddy talked with Grandma and Grandpa while Luke and Mother put the pancakes and the fruit on the plates. Suddenly Luke remembered one more thing. He opened the pantry and took out two walnuts. He broke the shells and crushed the nuts in his fingers. Then he sprinkled them on top of the yogurt on Grandpa's plate. Grandpa always asked for nuts on his sundae.

Luke looked at Grandpa's plate one more time before he served it. Everything was just right. It was piled high with two fluffy pancakes, maple syrup, a big mound of fresh berries and banana slices, and a giant scoop of vanilla yogurt with crushed nuts on top.

Luke carried the plate into the dining room and set it down in front of Grandpa. He watched Grandpa's eyes open wide. "My," was all Grandpa could say.

Luke took the note out of his pocket. "Here Grandpa," he said and handed him the envelope. "Read this first."

Grandpa pulled out the note card and read it out loud.

> Dear Grandpa,
>
> I made this pancake sundae just for you. Mr. Bartelli says it has all of the fun but none of the fat of an ice cream sundae. Too much fat is bad for your heart. I want you to live a long time.
> I love you, Grandpa.
>
> Luke

Luke watched Grandpa pull out a big white handkerchief. He wiped his eyes. Then he blew his nose.

Then he wiped his eyes again.

Grandpa took a big bite of Luke's pancake sundae. He rolled his eyes and smacked his lips. "Well, it looks like the Cold Spot just lost two good customers," he said and winked at Luke. "From now on after we play miniature golf, we're coming straight to your house, Luke. This pancake sundae beats a double-decker banana split any day."

Luke looked around the table. Everyone was smiling at him. Everyone except Grandpa. Grandpa was too busy eating his pancake sundae with nuts on top!

CREATE YOUR OWN PANCAKE SUNDAE

1. Make a batch of wholewheat or buckwheat pancakes.
   (Follow the directions on the box.)
2. Pour some real maple syrup into a pan and ask a grown-up to help you warm it on the stove.
3. Arrange cut, fresh fruit on a plate. (Bananas, kiwi, strawberries, or blueberries are the best.)
4. Scoop a container of vanilla yogurt into a bowl.
5. Chop up fresh walnuts or almonds.

Serve everyone a stack of pancakes. Let each one make his or her own pancake sundae using the ingredients above. Top with hot syrup. Yum!